Other giftbooks by Helen Exley:
The Best of Nature Quotations
Travel Notes and Quotes
Bon Voyage!
The Crazy World of Sailing

Published simultaneously in 1999 by Exley Publications Ltd
in Great Britain, and
Exley Publications LLC in the USA.

Copyright © Helen Exley 1999
The moral right of the author has been asserted.

12 11 10 9 8 7 6 5 4 3 2 1

ISBN 1-85015-994-7

Edited and pictures selected by Helen Exley.
Picture research by Image Select International.
Printed in China.

**Exley Publications Ltd, 16 Chalk Hill, Watford, Herts
WD1 4BN, UK.
Exley Publications LLC, 232 Madison Avenue, Suite 1206,
NY 10016, USA.**

THE CALL OF
THE
$\mathcal{S}$EA

A HELEN EXLEY GIFTBOOK

EXLEY
NEW YORK • WATFORD, UK

THALASSA! THE SEA!

The cry of the Greeks is somewhere in
every heart.
Thalassa!
The sea!
The first silver shining
– and our eyes lighten with joy.

PAM BROWN, B.1928

I must go; the sea has called me
As a mistress to her swain;
From the immemorial tumult
I shall drink of peace again.

F. O'NEILL GALLAGHER, FROM
"SEA MADNESS"

Whenever I find myself growing grim about
the mouth; whenever it is a damp, drizzly
November in my soul – then I account it high
time to get to sea as soon as I can.

HERMAN MELVILLE (1819-1891)

LET ME GO TO THE SEA AGAIN

Loose my bonds –

set me free –

Let me rise from my bed –

Let me go to the sea!

O! The sound of the sea.

DAPHNE DU MAURIER (1907-1989), FROM
"ENCHANTED CORNWALL"

Sister Sunlight, lead me then
Into thy healing seas again...

ALFRED NOYES (1880-1958),
FROM "MOODS OF THE SEA"

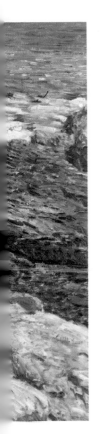

Exultation is the going
of an inland soul to sea,
Past the houses –
past the headlands –
into deep eternity –
Bred as we,
among the mountains,
Can the sailor understand
the divine intoxication
of the first league out
from land?

EMILY DICKINSON (1830-1886)

There is a society where
none intrudes,
By the deep sea, and music,
in its roar.

LORD BYRON (1788-1824),
FROM "CHILDE HAROLD'S PILGRIMAGE"

MY ROAD LEADS TO THE SEA

My road leads to shipping,
Where the bronzed sailors go.
Leads me, lures me, calls me
To salt green tossing sea....

JOHN MASEFIELD (1878-1967)

You have heard the beat of
the off-shore wind.
And the thresh of the
deep-sea rain;
You have heard the song –
how long? How long?
Pull out on the trail again!

RUDYARD KIPLING (1865-1936),
FROM "THE LONG TRAIL"

I must go down to the seas again
to the vagrant gypsy life,
To the gull's way and the whale's way
where the wind's like a whetted knife;
And all I ask is a merry yarn
from a laughing fellow-rover,
And quiet sleep and a sweet dream
when the long trick's over.

JOHN MASEFIELD (1878-1967),
FROM "SEA FEVER"

THE TOUCH OF THE SEA

The voice of the sea speaks to the soul. The touch of the sea is sensuous, enfolding the body in its soft, close embrace.

KATE CHOPIN (1851-1904),
FROM "THE AWAKENING"

Lie on the surface of a summer sea, out of the sight of land, under a cloudless sky – and feel the world beneath you, the depth of ocean, the circle of horizon.
People *must* live and work and love and weep *somewhere* on the planet – but silent, invisible. The earth and sea and sky hold only oneself, cocooned in a shimmer of silver light.

PAM BROWN, B.1928

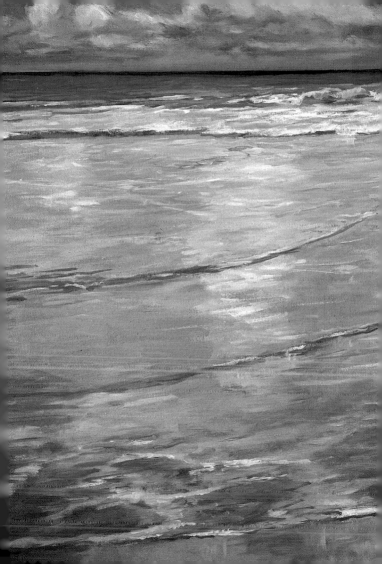

…Care slips away

Nowhere else than upon the sea do the days, weeks, and months fall away quicker into the past. They seem to be left astern as easily as the light air-bubbles in the swirls of the ship's wake.

JOSEPH CONRAD (1857-1924),
FROM "THE MIRROR OF THE SEA"

Wild white spray

It is a wonder foam is so beautiful.
A wave bursts in anger on a rock, broken up
in wild white sibilant spray and falls back,

drawing in its breath with rage, with frustration

how beautiful!

D.H. LAWRENCE (1885-1930)

The great sea has sent me adrift

The great sea

has sent me adrift.

It moves me as the weed

in a great river.

Earth and the great weather

move me,

have carried me away,

and move my inward parts

with joy.

UVAVNUK, AN ESKIMO SHAMAN
WOMAN, FROM "ESKIMO SONG"

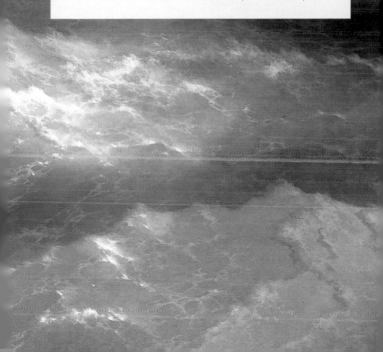

THE OCEAN IS A WILDERNESS REACHING
ROUND THE GLOBE, WILDER THAN A BENGAL
JUNGLE, AND FULLER OF MONSTERS,
WASHING THE VERY WHARVES OF OUR CITIES
AND THE GARDENS OF OUR SEA-SIDE
RESIDENCES.

HENRY DAVID THOREAU (1817-1862)

My road leads me seaward to white dipping sails.

JOHN MASEFIELD
(1878-1967)

The childhood mixture of excitement and apprehension was making the adrenalin flow and as I met the first scent of the sea, sharp, tangy and heavy with a fish-like smell, I was reminded of oceans green with plankton and of long Atlantic voyages. There is a subtle moment when the land and all its complexities are forgotten and the sea, in all its simplicity, stretches challengingly ahead.

CLARE FRANCIS,
FROM "THE
COMMANDING SEA"

WANDERLUST

I am fevered with the sunset,
I am fretful with the bay,
For the wander-thirst is on me
And my soul is in Cathay.

RICHARD HOVEY,
FROM "THE SEA GYPSY"

Journeys. Even the word sounds
as if it has been drawn from
some magic elixir and
distilled through the gossamer
screen of the imagination.

PHYLLIS TAYLOR PIANKA

It is very difficult to say where a
voyage begins. First of course
there must be a dream, a longing
for out-of-the-way places.

PETER HAMILTON, B.1922, FROM
"THE RESTLESS WIND"

Adventure!

The first experience can never be repeated. The
first love, the first sun-rise, the first South Sea
Island, are memories apart, and touched
a virginity of sense.

ROBERT LOUIS STEVENSON
(1850-1894), FROM "IN THE
SOUTH SEAS"

I love to sail forbidden seas, and land on barbarous coasts.

HERMAN MELVILLE (1819-1891)
FROM "MOBY DICK"

The romantic – that was what I wanted. I hungered for the romance of the sea, and foreign ports, and foreign smiles. I wanted to follow the prow of a ship, any ship, and sail away, perhaps to China, perhaps to Spain, perhaps to the South Sea Isles, there to do nothing all day long but lie on a surf-swept beach....

RICHARD HALLIBURTON (1900-1939)

MORBID THOUGHTS, GREY-GREEN GLOOM, LONGINGS FOR DEATH CHANGE ALMOST INSTANTANEOUSLY TO A SENSATION OF EXCITEMENT AND SPEED.... RAINBOW-TINTED SPRAY FLIES AROUND AND YOU KNOW THE ELATION ON TEARING THROUGH YOUR OWN BEJEWELLED PARADISE, FREE OF ALL MANKIND.

ANITA LESLIE, FROM "LOVE IN A NUTSHELL"

GIVE ME THIS GLORIOUS OCEAN LIFE

Give me this glorious ocean life, this salt-sea

life, this briny, foamy life, when the sea neighs

and snorts, and you breathe the very breath

that the great whales respire! Let me roll around

the globe, let me rock upon the sea;

let me race and pant out my life, with an

eternal breeze astern, and an endless sea before!

HERMAN MELVILLE (1819-1891)

Story of the earth

For thousands upon thousands of years the

sunlight and the sea and the masterless winds

have held tryst together.

LLEWELYN POWYS (1884-1939)

In every out-thrust headland,
in every curving beach, in
every grain of sand there is
a story of the earth.

RACHEL CARSON (1907-1964)

The sea drowns out humanity and time: it has
no sympathy with either, for it belongs to
eternity, and of that it sings its monotonous
song for ever and ever.

OLIVER WENDELL HOLMES (1809-1894),
FROM "THE AUTOCRAT OF THE BREAKFAST-TABLE"

A Water World

In the artificial world of his [man's] cities and towns, he often forgets the true nature of his planet and the long vistas of its history, in which existence of the race of men has occupied a mere moment of time. The sense of all these things comes to him most clearly in the course of a long ocean voyage, when he watches day after day the receding rim of the horizon, ridged and furrowed by waves; when at night he becomes aware of the earth's rotation as the stars pass overhead; or when, alone in this world of water and sky, he feels the loneliness of his earth in space. And then, as never on land, he knows the truth that his world is a water world, a planet dominated by its covering mantle of ocean, in which the continents are but transient intrusions of land above the surface of the all-encircling sea.

RACHEL CARSON (1907-1964),
FROM "THE SEA AROUND US"

How inappropriate to call
this planet Earth when
clearly it is Ocean.

ARTHUR CLARKE, B.1917

What is it in the sea life which is so powerful
in its influence?... It whispers in the wind of the
veldt, it hums in the music of the tropical night.
To some it is borne on the booming night-notes
of the deep forest, to others it speaks on the
silent snow peaks. But above all it is there to

the man who holds the night-watch alone at
sea. It is the sense of things done, of things
endured, of meanings not understood: the
secret of the Deep Silence, which is of eternity,
which the heart cannot speak.

H. WARINGTON SMYTH,
FROM "MAST AND SAIL"

Free!

One is free at last – and lilting in a slow flight of the elements, winging outwards. Oh, God, to be free of all the hemmed-in life – the horror of human tension, the absolute insanity of machine persistence. The agony which a train is to me, really. And the long-drawn-out agony of a life among tense, resistant people on land. And then to feel the long, slow lift and drop of this almost empty ship, as she took the waters. Ah, God, liberty, liberty, elemental liberty. I wished in my soul the voyage might last for ever, that the sea had no end, that one might float in this wavering, tremulous, yet long and surging pulsation while ever time lasted: space never exhausted, and no turning back, no looking back, even.

D.H. LAWRENCE (1885-1930),
FROM "SEA AND SARDINIA"

"THEY LOOK OUT TO SEA..."

The people along the sand
All turn and look one way.

They turn their back on the land.
They look at the sea all day.

ROBERT FROST (1874-1963),
FROM "NEITHER OUT FAR NOR IN DEEP"

One becomes
empty as the beach

Rollers on the beach, wind in the pines, the

slow flapping of herons across sand dunes,

frown out the hectic rhythms of city and

suburb, time tables and schedules. One falls

under their spell, relaxes, stretches out prone.

One becomes, in fact, like the element on

which one lies, flattened by the sea; bare, open,

empty as the beach, erased by today's tides of

all yesterday's scribblings.

ANNE MORROW LINDBERGH, B.1906,
FROM "GIFT FROM THE SEA"

THE EVER-CHANGING SEA

You can say it is blue, and even as you define the color it has turned to purple, or green, or gray, or black, or violet, and back to blue again. You can say it is restless, and while you speak the wind drops, the swells subside and from horizon to horizon there is no ripple, no flaw, no movement, only a vast sheet of pallid satin color. You can say it is calm and it rises and sweeps your coast cities away, throws your ships ashore, washes the keels of the flying clouds above. At the last, when you have sailed long enough and far enough, you come to understand that the sea is everything. It is calm and restless, stormy and laughing, many-hued and one-colored, salty and fresh, warm and cold, an enemy and a friend, a help and a hindrance, a tragedy and a jest. Everything! Sufficient for every mood, for every dream, for every hope, for every sorrow.

ALBERT RICHARD WETJEN (1900-1940),
FROM "WAY FOR A SAILOR!"

SHE CAN BE CRUEL

The sea is the one thing
that can never, even for
a moment, be taken
for granted.

GAVIN MAXWELL

You don't challenge the sea, or defy her. You listen, try to feel her mood if you can, and guess what she will do. You can love her, passionately, but she can make you afraid, and harm you; she can be cruel. Even when you think you know her, you can never tell what she has in store for you.

FRANCE AND CHRISTIAN GUILLAIN,
FROM "CALL OF THE SEA"

THE ANGRY SEA

AN ANGRY SEA ROARS ITS APPROACH,

GNAWS WITH GREY FANGS THE

HELPLESS SHORE.

TEARS AT THE CLIFF FACE –

BRINGS IT HURTLING DOWN

TO BE DEVOURED.

THINGS MAN HAD INTENDED

TO LAST A THOUSAND YEARS

SPLINTERED TO SHARDS

GROUND INTO SAND

AND ANONYMITY.

PAM BROWN. B.1928

And the storm went on. It roared, it bellowed,
and it screeched. it thumped and it
kerwhalloped. The great seas would come
bum agin the rocks, as if they were bound to
go right through to Jersey City, which they
used to say was the end of the world.

LAURA HOWE RICHARDS (1850-1943), FROM
"CAPTAIN JANUARY"

Eternal rhythms

The waters of the sea run through our
fingers, gentle over skin, sing to us in
moonlight, refresh our summer days.
Tear down cliff, castle, church and home.
Devour the land.
Grind all to little pebbles and to sand.

PAM BROWN. B.1928

On all these shores there are echoes of past and future; of the flow of time, obliterating yet containing all that has gone before; of the sea's eternal rhythms – the tides, the beat of surf, the pressing rivers of the currents – shaping, changing, dominating; of the stream of life, flowing as inexorably as any ocean current, from past to unknown future. For as the shore configuration changes in the flow of time, the pattern of life changes, never static, never quite the same from year to year. Whenever the sea builds a new coast, waves of living creatures surge against it, seeking a foothold, establishing their colonies. And so we come to perceive life as a force as tangible as any of the physical realities of the sea, a force strong and purposeful, as incapable of being crushed or diverted from its ends as the rising tide.

RACHEL CARSON (1907-1964),
FROM "THE EDGE OF THE SEA"

TO SEA, TO SEA!

*The anchor heaves, the ship
swings free,
The sails swell full.
To sea, to sea!*

THOMAS LOVELL BEDDOES (1803-1849)
FROM "TO SEA"

...The sky o'erarches here, we feel the
undulating deck beneath our feet,
We feel the long pulsation, ebb and flow of
endless motion,
The tones of unseen mystery, the vague and
vast suggestions of the briny world, the
liquid-flowing syllables,
The perfume, the faint creaking of the
cordage, the melancholy rhythm,
The boundless vista and the horizon far
and dim are all here,
And this is ocean's poem.

WALT WHITMAN (1819-1892),
FROM "IN CABIN'D SHIPS AT SEA"

That long, slow, waveringly rhythmic rise
and fall of the ship, with waters snorting as
it were from her nostrils, oh, God, what a
joy it is to the wild innermost soul.

D.H. LAWRENCE (1885-1930),
FROM "SEA AND SARDINIA"

Yourself and the boat and the sea

It is a complete world in itself, just yourself and the boat and the sea – a way of life almost, for you are on your own, entirely self-sufficient.

HAMMOND INNES. FROM "HARVEST OF JOURNEYS"

A sailing ship, however large, however small, talks to herself – and by the end of a lone night-watch you almost understand what she is saying.

The tip-tapping of the reef points, the sudden snapping of her canvas as you miscalculate a breeze. A humming in the rigging, a creaking of timbers. The water

chuckling at her prow, chopping against her
hull. The blocks protest, and rain and spray
patter against your oil skins.
And there are voices above you, all about you –
a conversation half heard, half translated – just
beyond your grasp.
You leave the sea, accept the land as home –
but never forget the shift of deck and spars and
rigging. The whispering in the shrouds. The
sound and scent and feel of this living creature.
For this was the she who answered to your
touch, or sulked or quibbled. A creature you
coaxed and scolded. A creature that you
praised: For she was an extension of your mind,
and you of hers. Ship, human soul and sinew
and the changing sea. All one. All moving as a
single entity.
Whatever her wilfulness, she has your heart
forever – and will never let you go.

PAM BROWN, B.1928

EVERY DAY IS THE SAME YET
DIFFERENT. IT REMINDS ME VERY
MUCH OF THE DESERT. THERE'S
JUST SOMETHING ABOUT THE
ENDLESS MILES AND MILES OF
ISOLATION THAT DRAWS YOU TO
ITS SOUL. I CAN'T IMAGINE EVER
BEING BORED OUT HERE. LIFE
TAKES ON A DIFFERENT MEANING.

LISA CLAYTON, FROM "AT THE
MERCY OF THE SEA"

I still experience that intoxicating mixture of fear and fascination which, despite many temptations to remain landbound, always lures me back for just one more voyage.

CLARE FRANCIS, FROM "THE COMMANDING SEA"

The feet of a seaman never forget the deck. The hands of a seaman never forget the ropes. The eyes of a seaman search the horizon for ever and a day.

PAM BROWN, B.1928

Called back to the sea

... deciding that I had come to the end of the road, I wrote a note to the boatyard, putting my boat up for sale. I said I was "coming off the water". But as I typed the sentence, I doubted that I meant a word of it. If no buyer turns up, I know what will happen: I will instruct the yard to put her in again – "just till somebody comes along". And then there will be the old uneasiness, the old uncertainty, as the mild south-east breeze ruffles the cove, a gentle, steady, morning breeze, bringing the taint of the distant wet world.... There will lie the sloop, there will blow the wind, once more I will get under way.

E.B. WHITE (1899-1985).
FROM "THE SEA AND THE
WIND THAT BLOWS"

The sea still held me

After a time at sea, I married, moved inland,
became subject to new demands – and thought
I had forgotten.

But we took the child to the coast one summer,
and walked along a harbour wall. And I heard
an anchor cable run through the hawse and was
caught again. How could the heart leap so, after
so long a time? How could I feel a deck under
my feet and the wheel under my hand, see the
great seas curving down astern and hear the
voices in the shrouds?

How could I long to leave all that I had – to see
once more the loom of lights across a moving
darkness, to feel the triumph of a landfall?

To see the storming petrels fluttering in our
wake, the glitter of phosphorescence,
the shifting colours of a dawn at sea?

Only a moment. My children called me.
Love took my arm.
But the sea smiled, knowing it still held me
– and would forever.

PAM BROWN, B.1928

The smell of rope and resin

Never a ship sails
out of the bay
But carries my heart
as a stowaway.

ROSELLE MONTGOMERY,
FROM "THE STOWAWAY"

As music flexes a dancer's muscles, even in old age, so the sounds of a ship bring back the longing to up anchor and leave the land behind.

PAM BROWN, B.1928

... I loved the smell of rope and resin, even of diesel oil. I loved the sound of water slapping hulls, the whip of halyards against tall masts. These were the scents and sounds of liberty and life.

ROBIN LEE GRAHAM, B.1949, FROM "DOVE"

I LOVE THE SEA AS I DO MY OWN SOUL.

HEINRICH HEINE (1797-1856)

I WAS SET FREE! I DISSOLVED...

I was set free! I dissolved in the sea, became
white sails and flying spray, became beauty and
rhythm, became moonlight and the ship and
the high dim-starred sky! I belonged, without

past or future, within peace and unity and a wild joy, within something greater than my own life, or the life of man, to Life itself!

EUGENE O'NEILL (1888-1953), FROM "LONG DAY'S JOURNEY INTO NIGHT"

INTO THE HEART, INTO THE MEMORY

A gentle,

scintillating sea

under a sky of wild

ducks and thin, high

cloud, washes into

the inlets,

into the heart,

into the memory.

PAM BROWN, B.1928

... the sea, once it casts its spell, holds one in its net of wonder forever.

JACQUES COUSTEAU, B.1919

THE GLORIOUS SEA

Give me the

sunlight and

the sea

And who shall

take my heaven

from me?

ALFRED NOYES (1880-1958).
FROM "MOOD OF THE SEA"

Acknowledgements: The publishers are grateful for permission to reproduce copyright material. Whilst every reasonable effort has been made to trace copyright holders, the publishers would be pleased to hear from any not here acknowledged. RACHEL CARSON: From *The Edge of The Sea,* published by Houghton Mifflin © 1955 R.L.Carson, renewed 1983 by Roger Christie reprinted with permission of Penguin Books. RACHEL CARSON : From *The Sea Around Us* published by Oxford University Press Inc. © 1951 R.L.Carson. DAPHNE DU MAURIER: From *Enchanted Cornwall,* with permission of Curtis Brown London Ltd, on behalf of The Chichester Partnership. © Daphne Du Maurier. CLARE FRANCIS: From *The Commanding Sea,* with permission of BBC Worldwide Ltd. © 1980 Nexus Communications Ltd. ROBERT FROST: From *Neither Far Out Nor In Deep* from The Poetry of Robert Frost. FRANCE AND CHRISTIAN GUILLAIN: From *Call of the Sea,* published by Gollancz 1976 © Editions Laffont, SA 1974. English translation © Caroline Hillier 1976. RUDYARD KIPLING: From *The Long Trail* with permission of A. P. Watt Ltd on behalf of the National Trust for Places of Historic Interest or Natural Beauty. D. H. LAWRENCE: From SEA AND SARDINIA and SPRAY with permission of Laurence Pollinger Ltd and the Estate of Frieda Lawrence Ravagli. JOHN MASEFIELD: From *Sea Fever* and *Roadways* with permission of The Society of Authors as the Literary Representative of the Estate of John Masefield. H.WARINGTON SMYTH: From MAST AND SAIL published by John Murray Ltd 1906 © Nigel Warington Smyth. E.B.WHITE © 1963 From: *The Sea and Wind that Blows* from Essays of E.B.White © 1963 published by HarperCollins Inc.

Picture Credits: Exley Publications would like to thank the following organizations and individuals for permission to reproduce their pictures. Whilst every reasonable effort has been made to trace copyright holders, the publishers would be pleased to hear from any not here acknowledged. AISA, Alinari (A), Art Resource (AR), The Bridgeman Art Library (BAL), Bulloz (B), Giraudon